DATE DUE

JAN 26			

242   $15.00
CHR Christenson, Evelyn

What Happens When
Children Prav

DEMCO

This Book Was Donated
by

BRAELYN N. THOMPSON

ON HER

6th Birthday
January 5, 2,000

Kindergarten- Full Day

Mrs. Triemstra

Southwest Chicago
Christian Schools

JDØ-01422 © APCo.

Chariot Books is an imprint of Chariot Victor Publishing
Cook Communications, Colorado Springs, CO 80918
Cook Communications, Paris, Ontario
Kingsway Communications, Eastbourne, England

What Happens When Children Pray
© 1997 by Evelyn Christenson for text and Joy Dunn Keenan for illustrations

Unless otherwise indicated, Scripture quotations in this publication are from
the *Holy Bible, New International Version.* Copyright © 1973, 1978, 1984,
International Bible Society. Used by permission of Zondervan Publishing House.
All rights reserved.

Scriptures marked (KJV) taken from the King James Version of the Bible.

ISBN: 0-78140-047-3
CIP information available upon request.

Design: PAZ Design Group
Art Direction: Andrea Boven
Editing: Liz Morton Duckworth
First printing: 1997
Printed in Mexico

01 00 99 98 97   5 4 3 2 1

What Happens When
CHILDREN
PRAY

Learning to Talk and Listen to God

Evelyn Christenson
with Liz Duckworth

Illustrated by Joy Dunn Keenan

Chariot VICTOR
PUBLISHING
A DIVISION OF COOK COMMUNICATIONS

What happens when children pray? Wonderful things!

God wants His children to love Him and to talk to Him—every day and at any time. These stories and pictures will show you other children who have been learning about prayer, just like you.

Cindy knows that God hears and answers her prayers. She talks to God every day.

"Call to Me, and I will answer."

—JEREMIAH 33:3A

For Jonathan's dad's birthday, Jonathan wants to ask God for something special. "Dear God," he prays, "please bless my dad and give him the very best year ever."

"The Lord bless you

and keep you."

— NUMBERS 6:24

9

Crista listens quietly to God. He helps her know the right thing to do. Sometimes God speaks to her through His special book, the Bible. It is filled with important messages about how to make right choices.

"Blessed are those who hear the word of God and obey it."

— LUKE 11:28

James thinks about other people, and he asks God to help them, take care of them, and fix their problems— even Grandma's computer!

"If we ask anything according to God's will, He hears us."

— 1 JOHN 5:14

James and Jonathan are praying for their baby brother Peter. They ask God to help their brother grow up to be healthy and strong.

"The prayer of a righteous man is powerful and effective."

— JAMES 5:16B

Brett remembers that God is his loving Father in heaven. Brett thanks God for giving him so many good things: a home, a family, food to eat each day, and his puppy and kitten.

"In every thing give thanks."

—1 THESSALONIANS 5:18A, KJV

atthew knows when he does something wrong. Then he asks God to forgive him and to make his heart clean again.

"If we confess our sins, He is faithful and just and will forgive us our sins."

—1 JOHN 1:9

Jenna forgives others when she prays. Sometimes it's not easy to forgive—like when a friend has hurt her feelings. But Jenna knows forgiving that person is what Jesus told us to do.

"And forgive us our debts, just as we also have forgiven our debtors."

— MATTHEW 6:12

Kathy loves to tell her friends about Jesus. Kathy prays with her friends at school—for those friends who don't know Jesus yet—that they might get to know Jesus like she does.

"My heart's desire and prayer...
is that they may be saved."

— ROMANS 10:1

A Time to Be Forgiven

Jan's dad was a pastor. He would stand in the front of the church every Sunday and teach people about Jesus. He helped them learn to know and love God better.

The Sunday before Easter, Jan listened closely while her dad told all about Jesus. He told them that Jesus was God's only Son and how He came to earth as a tiny baby, growing up to teach people all about God's love.

Some people didn't want to listen to Jesus. Though Jesus was kind and good, they killed Him. He died on the cross because of all the bad things people did to disobey God. But three days later, God made Jesus come to life again!

God promised that anyone who believed in Jesus would be forgiven for the bad things they had done, and would get to live with Him in heaven some day.

That night, Jan lay in bed thinking about all the bad things she had done. Sometimes she didn't obey her mom and dad. Sometimes she was selfish. Sometimes she hurt her friends' feelings. Her heart felt heavy and tears trickled down her cheeks.

Soon Jan felt a warm hand on her hot, damp cheek.

"Honey, why are you crying?" asked her mom.

"I was remembering all the awful, awful naughty things I've done. Daddy said that Jesus had to die because of all my bad things," Jan sobbed.

Her mother hugged Jan and said, "God loves you Jan and wants to forgive you, and help you obey. Do you want to talk to God now, and ask Him to forgive you?"

Dear God,

    Please forgive me for all the naughty things I've done. Please clean up my heart and let Jesus come and live in my heart. I love you and want to obey you always.

After she prayed, Jan patted her cheeks. Her tears had dried, and she felt warm and happy inside. She knew her prayer would be the start of a special friendship with Jesus, one that would last for always.

That's a promise we can read in the Bible: "God so loved the world that he gave his one and only Son. Anyone who believes in him shall not perish but have eternal life," (JOHN 3:16).

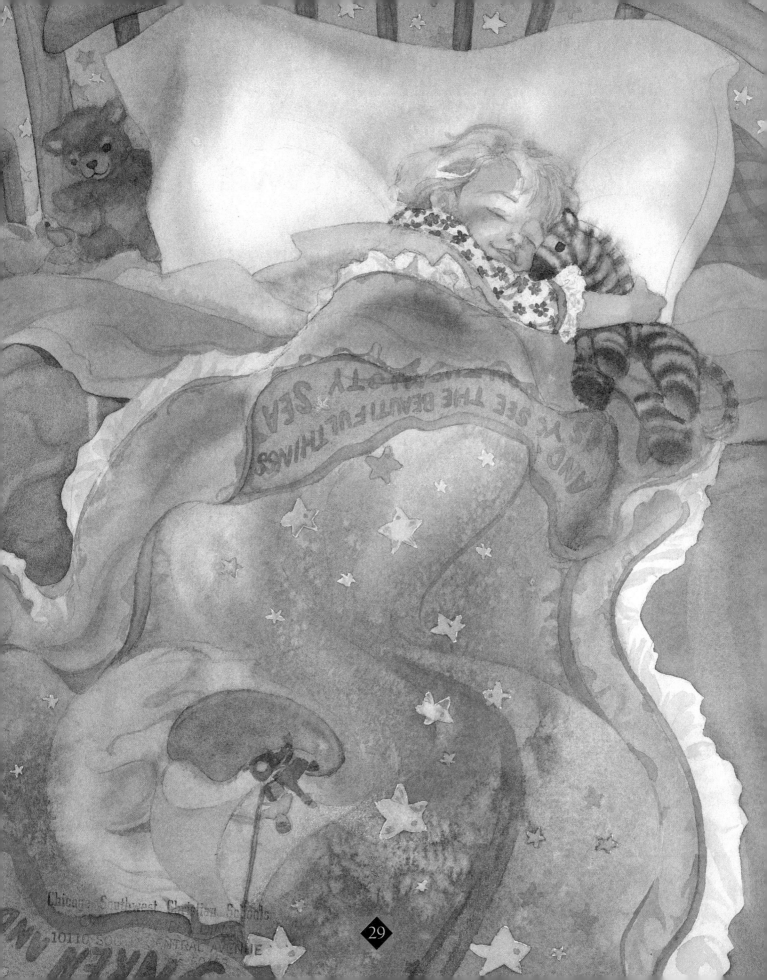

Ideas for Grownups

This book is designed to help children understand prayer and experience meaningful prayer times. Use it with children in your life and consider how you might bring these concepts home to each child, based on his or her age and personality. Here are some more ideas to help you do that effectively.

Go through the book slowly. Read each prayer and let your child practice it immediately.

As you work through the examples in this book, you may want to encourage your child to memorize the Scripture passages which are linked to the stories. Review these Scriptures whenever the future need arises. Young children have a wonderful capacity for memorization, and these reminders will return to them again and again as they grow in a relationship with God.

Methods of prayer that are effective with children:

Take-turn prayers—Keep prayer time with children as simple as possible. Try using sentence prayers in pairs or small groups. Each person takes a turn talking to God, limiting themselves to a single statement or request. Long, run-on prayers might become confusing to young children who often have short attention spans.

Criss-cross prayers—It's important for children to realize that grownups need prayer too. Allow your child to pray for you, just as you pray for that child. You might want to draw a picture of an "X" as a picture of a "criss-cross prayer" where each prays for the other.

Front-door prayers—In some families, mornings are busy, stressful times. Before each family member departs for school or work, pause a moment at the front door praying about their day. Ask the Lord to protect and guide, so that children are reassured that they are not going out to meet the world alone, but they are going out under God's care.

Touching prayers—Most children love to cuddle and hug. There is a wonderful opportunity during these times of closeness, to bring God into the picture, in a concrete way for little ones. Next time you share the love of a hug with your child, try praying also, adding God's presence and influence to the loving arms encircling that child.